JOURNALLING THROUGH
GENESIS

WITH
THE DEVOTED COLLECTIVE

The Devoted Collective
Auckland, New Zealand
www.thedevotedcollective.org

© Copyright 2021 The Devoted Collective Ltd. All rights reserved.

ISBN: 978-0-473-61374-7

No portion of this book may be reproduced, stored in a retrieval system or transmitted in any form or by any means—electronic, mechanical, photocopy, recording or otherwise— except for brief quotations in printed reviews of promotion, without prior written permission from the author. All text in bold or in parentheses are the author's own.

Unless otherwise noted, all Scripture is taken from the New International Version®, NIV®. Copyright © 1973, 1978, 1984, 2011 by Biblica, Inc.™ Used by permission of Zondervan. All rights reserved worldwide.

Cover design by Holly Robertson of Design by Rocket www.designbyrocket.com
Book Illustrations by Marie Warner Preston of Outspoken Images www.outspokenimages.com
Compiled by Aimée Walker
Edited by Ellie Di Julio

Cataloguing in Publishing Data Title: Reading Through Genesis
Author: The Devoted Collective
Subjects: Devotions, Christian life, Spirituality

A copy of this title is held at the National Library of New Zealand

In the beginning...

The book of Genesis opens with the words, "In the beginning God created," reminding us from the very outset that nothing about this life is random. This world–and each and every one of us–was fashioned with deliberate intention and imbued with divine purpose. It's a theme that we will revisit time and again as we read through this foundational book together: God has always been working to a plan. One that has stood firm since before the beginning of time and is explored and revealed throughout all of Scripture. A plan that absolutely nothing can derail– neither Fall nor Flood nor human weakness–for God's purposes will always prevail.

But Genesis does much more than simply introduce us to God's master plan; it also invites us to become an intimate part of it. From Noah to Abraham to Isaac, Jacob, and Joseph, we are continually reminded that, in spite of everything, God keeps choosing to partner with humanity; keeps choosing to redeem what sin has broken and marred in our lives, keeps showing us the extent of His loving kindness toward us.

And perhaps this is the most wondrous part of Genesis: that amidst all the mess and failing and the heaviness of sin's curse, the seed of the hope of redemption is firmly planted not only in the pages of Scripture, but also in our hearts. As we travel with those who first walked this earth, we see our stories reflected in theirs. Our own need for a Saviour is exposed, and our eyes are opened to see the beauty of all that Jesus offers us.

It is our prayer that, as you journal your way through Genesis with us, your understanding of Scripture will be expanded and enriched, the foundations of your faith strengthened, and your heart brought to a place of overflowing awe and gratitude for the goodness of our God.

The Devoted Team

Genesis in Context

To help you get the most out of your study of Genesis, we've compiled some background notes and tips for using this journal. Anchoring your observations in the correct historical and Scriptural context will enrich what you take away from your time in the Word and help you to build a solid theological foundation.

AUTHORSHIP

While Moses is not named in Genesis as its writer, rabbinic tradition attributes him as the sole author of the Torah—a tradition supported by Scripture itself (Exodus 17:4; Leviticus 1:1-2; Deuteronomy 1:1; Joshua 1:7; Matthew 8:4; Mark 12:26; Luke 16:29). However, unlike the other four books authored by Moses—Exodus, Leviticus, Numbers, and Deuteronomy—he is not an eyewitness to the events recorded in Genesis but rather the compiler of records and oral traditions passed down through the generations.

DATING

The events of Genesis span several thousand years, recording from the moment of Creation to the death of Joseph in approximately 1600 B.C. This is the broadest period covered in a single book of the Bible, which can seem daunting but also testifies to the steadfastness of God throughout history.

AUDIENCE

Moses was writing to a newly freed Israel, a people surrounded by enemy nations, who for hundreds of years had known nothing but slavery and suffering. By telling the story of their creation by Yahweh—the LORD, the God of Israel—and recording the lineages and stories of their ancestors, Moses was embedding in this nascent nation their identity as God's special covenant people, reminding them that they were still purposed for great things, despite their struggles.

This recounting of Israel's origins has application for us still today. As those who have also become Abraham's seed through faith in Jesus Christ (Galatians 3:26-29), our own identity is shaped by these events, and we are reminded that we have been grafted into a plan that spans generations and continues to draw people into covenant relationship with the Living God.

GENRE

Genesis is classified as historical narrative: Events from the past are retold for the benefit and guidance of another generation. But make no mistake, these stories should never be reduced to mythology, mere moral lessons, or simple allegories. These are true events whose primary purpose is to tell us what God did in the history of Israel. And herein lies the crucial difference between biblical narratives and other narratives: This is God's story—and He, not us, is always the hero.

When reading these accounts, it can be tempting to interpret them through our own cultural lens, judging them from our vantage point in history. But it is vital that we consider them in the context of the biblical authors, always remembering that they recorded events as they actually happened and not necessarily as they *should* have happened.

One of the things that can help us interpret this genre well is to keep God's universal plan in the forefront of our minds, asking the question: *How is the big picture story of redemption unfolding and how do the individual stories being told fit into it?*

STRUCTURE

Genesis can be divided into two basic parts: a pre-history (Chapters 1-11) and the story of the beginning of redemption through Abraham and his seed (Chapters 12-50). In the first section, the focus is on the beginnings of the human race. Four major events spanning approximately 2000 years are honed in on: Creation (1-2:25); the Fall (3:1-5:32); the Flood (6:1-9:29), and the Nations (10:1-11:9). In the second section, the style becomes more biographical, exploring the origins of Israel through four key people across roughly 193 years: Abraham, Isaac, Jacob, and Joseph.

A secondary structure within Genesis is what is known as a 'toldot structure'—a literary construction built on generations. This structure begins in Genesis 2:4 with the first human family in the Garden of Eden and works successively through Noah and Shem, Terah and Abraham, Isaac and Jacob, and finally, Joseph—each story repeating the wonder that our holy, sovereign God chooses to partner with flawed humans to accomplish His purposes on earth. As you read, keep an eye out for the toldot phrasing of "this is the account of," as it signals a new development in the overall story. Within this structure, you'll discover that the family lines of the rejected sons (Cain, Ishmael, Esau) are also given. The contrast of their genealogies and legacies with that of the chosen sons is often stark and points us to the blessing that is found in living under God's care.

A further framing device creating structure is God's use of Noah in the early chapters of Genesis to preserve human life during the great deluge (Chapters 6-9) and of Joseph to preserve human life during the great drought in the final chapters (37-50). These stories become foundational structures, linking the whole of the Bible together into a unified story as they point us to the eventual entrance of Christ, the ultimate preserver of life.

THEMES

The major plot of Genesis is redemption; we continually witness a cycle of generation, degeneration, and regeneration. Each time humanity falls to a new low, God is faithful to forgive their shortcomings, intervening in the history of human fallenness and offering them a new beginning; He chooses to work with, rather than despite, man. Through Noah and the families of Abraham, Isaac, and Jacob, we see this overarching theme of redemption and numerous other key themes of Scripture being established.

Origins

The Hebrew name for this book is *Bereishit*, which means 'in the beginning,' while 'genesis' itself means 'book of origins.' Genesis is a record of the beginnings of Creation, humanity, sin, marriage, language, the nations, Israel, and so much more. In detailing all these origins, it establishes the historical and theological basis for Israel being God's chosen people and sets up how the Gentile nations will later be invited to become sons of Abraham and, therefore, sons of God.

We also see much of what is begun in Genesis continue to be developed throughout the narrative of Scripture before finding its final resolution in Revelation. For example, in Genesis, we have the creation of the first heaven and earth, while in Revelation, the new and eternal heaven and earth will be established. In Genesis, Satan tempts Eve to sin; in Revelation, he will be thrown into the fire. In Genesis, death enters the scene; in Revelation, there will be no more death or suffering. In Genesis, the Redeemer is promised; in Revelation, He will reign forever. This pattern reinforces the truth of God's unwavering plans and gives us confidence in the cohesiveness and trustworthiness of the Scriptures.

Curse of Sin

We not only see the origins of sin revealed in Genesis but also its long-term consequences throughout history. Connected to this theme is that of 'holy war.' This is God's special battle against evil and those who manifest it—a battle God fights on behalf of the righteous but allows His people to participate in. This theme begins with the curse on the serpent and is subtly picked up again in Genesis 12 with Abraham, setting up the conflict of the books of Exodus and Joshua where holy war will become a central focus.

Sovereignty of God

God speaks, and it comes into being. Though humanity repeatedly tries (and fails) to take control of matters, God's plans and purposes always prevail. His will is supreme, and He will accomplish all He intends, both in spite of and in conjunction with human weakness. He frequently chooses the younger, weaker, and most unlikely people to partner with—such as Seth, Isaac, and Jacob—as well as the perpetually flawed—such as Abram and Judah—reminding us that God can (and does) use anyone to accomplish His purposes.

Covenant Relationship

Throughout Genesis, covenant—a formal, binding agreement between parties, akin to a contract but more personal in nature—emerges as the basis of relationship between God and humanity. God establishes Himself as a covenant-keeper who faithfully upholds His promises, despite the perpetually covenant-breaking human race. Each covenant He makes points us to Christ, who will one day fulfill all of humanity's covenant requirements and establish the New Covenant in Himself, bringing God and His people together in true relationship, restoring the good purposes He intended from the first moment of Creation.

Genesis records the institution of

the first two explicit covenants: the Noahic (9:8-17) and Abrahamic (12:2-7, 15:1-21, 17:3-8). These share several features: Both are given during periods of decline, pointing to God's continual intervention and redemptive work on our behalf; each are given a sign to mark them (9:12-13, 17:11); and each are considered to be unconditional, their fulfilment not dependent upon human performance but upon God's grace and mercy.

Together with the Mosaic and Davidic covenants to come (Exodus 20-24, 2 Samuel 7), these initial covenants tell the story of God's redemptive plan, building up to the New Covenant under Jesus. By understanding these agreements and relationships, we are better able to see the incredible grace of God towards His creation that is revealed in Scripture.

SEEING JESUS IN GENESIS

Genesis invites us to witness the start of many things—Creation, humanity, sin, culture, and the nations, to name a few—but its greatest invitation is to glimpse the introduction of God's ultimate expression of love: Jesus. His coming as our Saviour and Redeemer is anticipated through:

Prophecies: Genesis 3:15, 12:3, 17:19, 28:14, 49:10

Types: Adam, Abel, Noah, Melchizedek, Isaac, Joseph

Genealogies: Genesis 5, 11

Christophanies: Genesis 16:7-14, 18, 22:11 18, 31:11 13, 32:22 32

From the Word of Creation to shadows of His character to timely appearances, Jesus is powerfully present in the Old Testament. As we read through this book of beginnings, let us ask the Holy Spirit to reveal Christ woven throughout humanity's ancient origins and lead us into greater understanding of His presence in our modern context.

How To Use This Journal

This journal is organised into twelve weeks of readings. Within each week, you'll find five days of readings and journalling pages, allowing two 'grace' days to catch up on any missed days and to reflect on what you've learned with our 'Week in Review' pages. The combination of lines and white space is designed to allow you to be creative in how you record your journey through Genesis. Illustrate a verse, ask the Spirit to draw with you, collage words that stand out—anything you feel moved to do!

Our journalling pages follow a pattern of *Observations, Obstacles,* and *Outcomes*. Start by reading the passage of Scripture in full. If you have time, consider going through it a few times to really get familiar with the nuances and details that are easily missed in a single pass. Once you have read the passage, you are ready to make your observations.

Observations:

God's Word is a rich treasure trove, and no matter how familiar a passage may feel, there is always something more for us to discover there. As you slow down to make your observations, invite the Holy Spirit to open the eyes of your heart and to give you insight and understanding. Then begin by noting the themes and connections you observe in the passage as a whole before working through verse by verse.

Questions you may find helpful to ask yourself:

When and where do these events take place?
Who is in this passage?
What is happening? *Why* is it happening?
How are repetition, contrast, wordplay, symbols, etc used to draw out meaning?
What themes are being developed?
What do these verses reveal about the character and nature of God?
Where is Jesus in this passage?

Obstacles:

This section is your space to wrestle. As we read and study Scripture, it's important that we don't gloss over the hard parts. We need to be honest with ourselves about what we don't understand, what we struggle to reconcile with what we know about God, what feels contradictory with other parts of the Bible, and what might be difficult to implement. If we don't voice these things, doubt can begin to erode the foundations of our faith.

Each day, we encourage you to record the things you've read that pose an obstacle for you—whether it's an issue of understanding or outworking. Then, if you need to do some research to understand more fully, research. If you need to sit with the Lord and let the Holy Spirit guide you, sit. Know that God is big enough to handle your questions and wants to empower you to walk in the truth of His Word. You might not always uncover the answers you're looking for immediately, but identifying the things you wrestle with starts the conversation and makes a space for the Holy Spirit to instruct you in this area.

Outcomes:

This is where we pause to consider the application of the passage in the context of our everyday lives. We don't want to simply consume information but to allow ourselves to be shaped and transformed by the words which ultimately point us to the Living Word: Christ. This will only happen if we recognise that God's Word is alive and active, understanding that while it has an intended application for its original audience, it also meets us where we are at today.

Take some time to reflect. *Is there something God is inviting you to do in response to what you have read? Something He is wanting to encourage you with at this time?* Write these things down and invite the Holy Spirit to show you how you can practically outwork them.

Using 'the 3 Os' to study and meditate on the Word will help you draw closer to the heart of the Father as your understanding of His character, good purposes, and sovereign plans is enriched. May each day's reflection deepen your relationship with the One who has loved you from the start of it all.

WEEK ONE
GENESIS 1-4

Day One

GENESIS 1:1-23

OBSERVATIONS

OBSTACLES

OUTCOMES

Day Two

GENESIS 1:24-2:3

OBSERVATIONS

OBSTACLES

OUTCOMES

Day Three

GENESIS 2:4-25

OBSERVATIONS

OBSTACLES

OUTCOMES

Day Four

GENESIS 3

OBSERVATIONS

OBSTACLES

OUTCOMES

Day Five

GENESIS 4

OBSERVATIONS

OBSTACLES

OUTCOMES

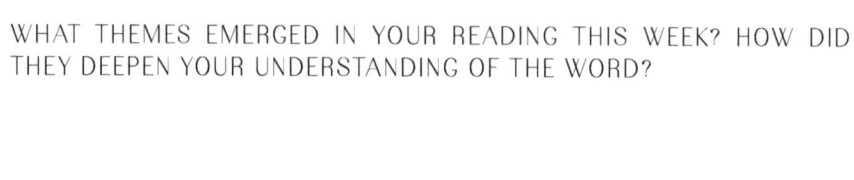

WHAT THEMES EMERGED IN YOUR READING THIS WEEK? HOW DID THEY DEEPEN YOUR UNDERSTANDING OF THE WORD?

HOW DID THE LORD ENCOURAGE AND CHALLENGE YOU THROUGH THIS WEEK'S READING?

WHICH OF YOUR 'OUTCOMES' IS GOD INVITING YOU TO PRIORITISE IN THE WEEK AHEAD? WHAT IS YOUR PART IN OUTWORKING IT?

WEEK TWO
GENESIS 5-9

Day Six

GENESIS 5

OBSERVATIONS

OBSTACLES

OUTCOMES

Day Seven

GENESIS 6

OBSERVATIONS

OBSTACLES

OUTCOMES

GENESIS 7

OBSERVATIONS

OBSTACLES

OUTCOMES

GENESIS 8

OBSERVATIONS

OBSTACLES

OUTCOMES

Day Ten

GENESIS 9

OBSERVATIONS

OBSTACLES

OUTCOMES

Week in Review

WHAT THEMES EMERGED IN YOUR READING THIS WEEK? HOW DID THEY DEEPEN YOUR UNDERSTANDING OF THE WORD?

HOW DID THE LORD ENCOURAGE AND CHALLENGE YOU THROUGH THIS WEEK'S READING?

WHICH OF YOUR 'OUTCOMES' IS GOD INVITING YOU TO PRIORITISE IN THE WEEK AHEAD? WHAT IS YOUR PART IN OUTWORKING IT?

WEEK THREE
GENESIS 10-14

Day Eleven

GENESIS 10

OBSERVATIONS

OBSTACLES

OUTCOMES

Day Twelve

GENESIS 11:1-9

OBSERVATIONS

OBSTACLES

OUTCOMES

Day Thirteen

GENESIS 11:10-12:9

OBSERVATIONS

OBSTACLES

OUTCOMES

Day Fourteen

GENESIS 12:10-13:18

OBSERVATIONS

OBSTACLES

OUTCOMES

Day Fifteen

GENESIS 14

OBSERVATIONS

OBSTACLES

OUTCOMES

Week in Review

WHAT THEMES EMERGED IN YOUR READING THIS WEEK? HOW DID THEY DEEPEN YOUR UNDERSTANDING OF THE WORD?

HOW DID THE LORD ENCOURAGE AND CHALLENGE YOU THROUGH THIS WEEK'S READING?

WHICH OF YOUR 'OUTCOMES' IS GOD INVITING YOU TO PRIORITISE IN THE WEEK AHEAD? WHAT IS YOUR PART IN OUTWORKING IT?

WEEK FOUR
GENESIS 15-18

Day Sixteen

GENESIS 15

OBSERVATIONS

OBSTACLES

OUTCOMES

Day Seventeen

GENESIS 16

OBSERVATIONS

OBSTACLES

OUTCOMES

Day Eighteen

GENESIS 17

OBSERVATIONS

OBSTACLES

OUTCOMES

Day Nineteen

GENESIS 18:1-15

OBSERVATIONS

OBSTACLES

OUTCOMES

Day Twenty

GENESIS 18:16-33

OBSERVATIONS

OBSTACLES

OUTCOMES

Week in Review

WHAT THEMES EMERGED IN YOUR READING THIS WEEK? HOW DID THEY DEEPEN YOUR UNDERSTANDING OF THE WORD?

HOW DID THE LORD ENCOURAGE AND CHALLENGE YOU THROUGH THIS WEEK'S READING?

WHICH OF YOUR 'OUTCOMES' IS GOD INVITING YOU TO PRIORITISE IN THE WEEK AHEAD? WHAT IS YOUR PART IN OUTWORKING IT?

WEEK FIVE
GENESIS 19-21

Day Twenty-One

GENESIS 19:1-29

OBSERVATIONS

OBSTACLES

OUTCOMES

Day Twenty-Two

GENESIS 19:30-38

OBSERVATIONS

OBSTACLES

OUTCOMES

Day Twenty-Three

GENESIS 20

OBSERVATIONS

OBSTACLES

OUTCOMES

Day Twenty-Four

GENESIS 21:1-21

OBSERVATIONS

OBSTACLES

OUTCOMES

Day Twenty-Five

GENESIS 21:22-34

OBSERVATIONS

OBSTACLES

OUTCOMES

Week in Review

WHAT THEMES EMERGED IN YOUR READING THIS WEEK? HOW DID THEY DEEPEN YOUR UNDERSTANDING OF THE WORD?

HOW DID THE LORD ENCOURAGE AND CHALLENGE YOU THROUGH THIS WEEK'S READING?

WHICH OF YOUR 'OUTCOMES' IS GOD INVITING YOU TO PRIORITISE IN THE WEEK AHEAD? WHAT IS YOUR PART IN OUTWORKING IT?

WEEK SIX
GENESIS 22–25

Day Twenty-Six

GENESIS 22

OBSERVATIONS

OBSTACLES

OUTCOMES

Day Twenty-Seven

GENESIS 23

OBSERVATIONS

OBSTACLES

OUTCOMES

Day Twenty-Eight

GENESIS 24:1-27

OBSERVATIONS

OBSTACLES

OUTCOMES

Day Twenty-Nine

GENESIS 24:28-67

OBSERVATIONS

OBSTACLES

OUTCOMES

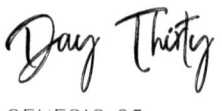

GENESIS 25

OBSERVATIONS

OBSTACLES

OUTCOMES

Week in Review

WHAT THEMES EMERGED IN YOUR READING THIS WEEK? HOW DID THEY DEEPEN YOUR UNDERSTANDING OF THE WORD?

HOW DID THE LORD ENCOURAGE AND CHALLENGE YOU THROUGH THIS WEEK'S READING?

WHICH OF YOUR 'OUTCOMES' IS GOD INVITING YOU TO PRIORITISE IN THE WEEK AHEAD? WHAT IS YOUR PART IN OUTWORKING IT?

WEEK SEVEN
GENESIS 26-29

Day Thirty-One

GENESIS 26

OBSERVATIONS

OBSTACLES

OUTCOMES

Day Thirty-Two

GENESIS 27:1-29

OBSERVATIONS

OBSTACLES

OUTCOMES

Day Thirty-Three

GENESIS 27:30-46

OBSERVATIONS

OBSTACLES

OUTCOMES

Day Thirty-Four

GENESIS 28

OBSERVATIONS

OBSTACLES

OUTCOMES

Day Thirty-Five

GENESIS 29

OBSERVATIONS

OBSTACLES

OUTCOMES

Week in Review

WHAT THEMES EMERGED IN YOUR READING THIS WEEK? HOW DID THEY DEEPEN YOUR UNDERSTANDING OF THE WORD?

HOW DID THE LORD ENCOURAGE AND CHALLENGE YOU THROUGH THIS WEEK'S READING?

WHICH OF YOUR 'OUTCOMES' IS GOD INVITING YOU TO PRIORITISE IN THE WEEK AHEAD? WHAT IS YOUR PART IN OUTWORKING IT?

WEEK EIGHT
GENESIS 30-32:21

GENESIS 30:1-24

OBSERVATIONS

OBSTACLES

OUTCOMES

Day Thirty-Seven

GENESIS 30:25-43

OBSERVATIONS

OBSTACLES

OUTCOMES

Day Thirty-Eight

GENESIS 31:1-21

OBSERVATIONS

OBSTACLES

OUTCOMES

# Day Thirty-Nine

GENESIS 31:22-55

OBSERVATIONS

OBSTACLES

OUTCOMES

Day Forty

GENESIS 32:1-21

OBSERVATIONS

OBSTACLES

OUTCOMES

Week in Review

WHAT THEMES EMERGED IN YOUR READING THIS WEEK? HOW DID THEY DEEPEN YOUR UNDERSTANDING OF THE WORD?

HOW DID THE LORD ENCOURAGE AND CHALLENGE YOU THROUGH THIS WEEK'S READING?

WHICH OF YOUR 'OUTCOMES' IS GOD INVITING YOU TO PRIORITISE IN THE WEEK AHEAD? WHAT IS YOUR PART IN OUTWORKING IT?

WEEK NINE
GENESIS 32:22 - GENESIS 36

Day Forty-One

GENESIS 32:22-32

OBSERVATIONS

OBSTACLES

OUTCOMES

Day Forty-Two

GENESIS 33

OBSERVATIONS

OBSTACLES

OUTCOMES

Day Forty-Three

GENESIS 34

OBSERVATIONS

OBSTACLES

OUTCOMES

Day Forty-Four

GENESIS 35

OBSERVATIONS

OBSTACLES

OUTCOMES

Day Forty-Five

GENESIS 36

OBSERVATIONS

OBSTACLES

OUTCOMES

WHAT THEMES EMERGED IN YOUR READING THIS WEEK? HOW DID THEY DEEPEN YOUR UNDERSTANDING OF THE WORD?

HOW DID THE LORD ENCOURAGE AND CHALLENGE YOU THROUGH THIS WEEK'S READING?

WHICH OF YOUR 'OUTCOMES' IS GOD INVITING YOU TO PRIORITISE IN THE WEEK AHEAD? WHAT IS YOUR PART IN OUTWORKING IT?

WEEK TEN
GENESIS 37-41:36

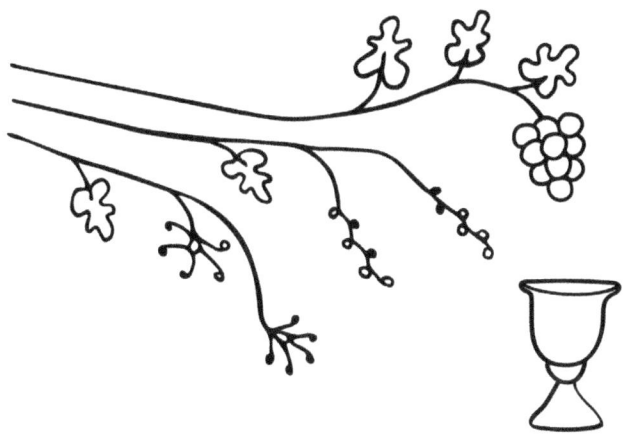

Day Forty-Six

GENESIS 37

OBSERVATIONS

OBSTACLES

OUTCOMES

Day Forty-Seven

GENESIS 38

OBSERVATIONS

OBSTACLES

OUTCOMES

Day Forty-Eight

GENESIS 39

OBSERVATIONS

OBSTACLES

OUTCOMES

Day Forty-Nine

GENESIS 40

OBSERVATIONS

OBSTACLES

OUTCOMES

Day Fifty

GENESIS 41:1-36

OBSERVATIONS

OBSTACLES

OUTCOMES

Week in Review

WHAT THEMES EMERGED IN YOUR READING THIS WEEK? HOW DID THEY DEEPEN YOUR UNDERSTANDING OF THE WORD?

HOW DID THE LORD ENCOURAGE AND CHALLENGE YOU THROUGH THIS WEEK'S READING?

WHICH OF YOUR 'OUTCOMES' IS GOD INVITING YOU TO PRIORITISE IN THE WEEK AHEAD? WHAT IS YOUR PART IN OUTWORKING IT?

WEEK ELEVEN
GENESIS 41:37 - GENESIS 45

Day Fifty-One

GENESIS 41:37-57

OBSERVATIONS

OBSTACLES

OUTCOMES

Day Fifty-Two

GENESIS 42

OBSERVATIONS

OBSTACLES

OUTCOMES

Day Fifty-Three

GENESIS 43

OBSERVATIONS

OBSTACLES

OUTCOMES

Day Fifty-Four

GENESIS 44

OBSERVATIONS

OBSTACLES

OUTCOMES

Day Fifty-Five

GENESIS 45

OBSERVATIONS

OBSTACLES

OUTCOMES

Week in Review

WHAT THEMES EMERGED IN YOUR READING THIS WEEK? HOW DID THEY DEEPEN YOUR UNDERSTANDING OF THE WORD?

HOW DID THE LORD ENCOURAGE AND CHALLENGE YOU THROUGH THIS WEEK'S READING?

WHICH OF YOUR 'OUTCOMES' IS GOD INVITING YOU TO PRIORITISE IN THE WEEK AHEAD? WHAT IS YOUR PART IN OUTWORKING IT?

WEEK TWELVE
GENESIS 46-50

Day Fifty-Six

GENESIS 46

OBSERVATIONS

OBSTACLES

OUTCOMES

Day Fifty-Seven

GENESIS 47

OBSERVATIONS

OBSTACLES

OUTCOMES

Day Fifty-Eight

GENESIS 48

OBSERVATIONS

OBSTACLES

OUTCOMES

Day Fifty-Nine

GENESIS 49

OBSERVATIONS

OBSTACLES

OUTCOMES

Day Sixty

GENESIS 50

OBSERVATIONS

OBSTACLES

OUTCOMES

Week in Review

WHAT THEMES EMERGED IN YOUR READING THIS WEEK? HOW DID THEY DEEPEN YOUR UNDERSTANDING OF THE WORD?

HOW DID THE LORD ENCOURAGE AND CHALLENGE YOU THROUGH THIS WEEK'S READING?

WHICH OF YOUR 'OUTCOMES' IS GOD INVITING YOU TO PRIORITISE IN THE WEEK AHEAD? WHAT IS YOUR PART IN OUTWORKING IT?

Our vision is simple: to serve God with wholehearted devotion, fulfilling the command Christ gave us to love the Lord with all our heart, soul, and mind (Matthew 22:37).

We want to love God with all that we are right where we are. In order to do that, The Devoted Collective is anchored in three core disciplines modelled for us in Acts 2:42: devotion to the Word, to community, and to prayer. It is our heart's desire that, through committing to these practices with us, you will experience the richness of all God intends for your life as you come to know Him more intimately.

The more we know God, the more we can't help but love Him; and the more we love Him, the more we'll desire to partner with Him to establish it on earth as it is in Heaven. And that's what wholehearted devotion is all about.

CONNECT WITH US

@thedevotedcollective
www.thedevotedcollective.org

www.ingramcontent.com/pod-product-compliance
Lightning Source LLC
Chambersburg PA
CBHW072007290426
44109CB00018B/2161